Retention Theory for Teachers

MADELINE HUNTER

University of California, Los Angeles

D1601083

CORWIN PRESS, INC.
A Sage Publications Company
Thousand Oaks, California

Other publications by the same author:

Mastery Teaching
Motivation Theory for Teachers
Discipline That Develops Self-Discipline
Teach More — Faster!
Teach for Transfer
Aide-ing in Education
Improved Instruction
Improving Your Child's Behavior
Parent-Teacher Conferencing
Mastering Coaching and Supervision

Retention Theory for Teachers
© Copyright 1967 by Madeline Hunter

Printed in the United States of America.
98 99 00 01 02 03 04 05 46 45 44 43 42 41 40 39

Hunter, Madeline C.
    Retention theory for teachers / Madeline Hunter.
        p.   cm.
    Originally published: El Segundo, Calif. : TIP Publications, c 1967.
    ISBN 0-8039-6316-5   (pbk. : alk. paper)
1. Memory.   2. Learning, Psychology of .   I. Title.
LB1063.H86   1995
370.15'22 — dc20   95-6569

For information on the complete Madeline Hunter Collection, please contact:

CORWIN PRESS, INC.
A Sage Publications Company
2455 Teller Road
Thousand Oaks, CA 91320-2218
Call: 805-499-9774 Fax: 805-499-0871

FOREWORD

Psychological knowledge that will result in sign.ficantly increased learning of students is now available for teachers. In most cases, this knowledge remains unused because it is written in language that takes an advanced statistician to decode, or is buried in research journals in university libraries.

This book is one of a series written to make this important knowledge available to the classroom teacher. As such it makes no attempt to achieve comprehensive coverage of the subject, but endeavors to interpret that knowledge which is most useful in the daily decisions of teachers. The purist in learning theory may complain that some generalizations are over-simplified. Our answer would be that understanding a theory in simple form is necessary to the desire to search for increasing ramifications and complexities. The reader must also be warned that decisions based on learning theory are decisions of HOW to teach. These decisions can be made only AFTER the teacher has made decisions of WHAT content to teach and WHICH objectives are appropriate for the learner in that content area.

In other words, once a teacher has identified an appropriate educational destination for the learner, knowledge of learning theory will reveal the most effective, efficient and economical route to reach that destination.

Appreciation is expressed to the professors who made psychological theory meaningful to me when I was a student, to Dr. May Seagoe who encouraged me with her belief that it is important for all teachers, to Mrs. Margaret Devers and Mrs. Elsa Gilbert whose ability to decode my writing made a manuscript possible, and to the many teachers I have trained who continually reaffirmed my belief that there is nothing more practical than a valid theory.

Madeline Hunter

To my family who survived it, this
book is affectionately dedicated.

RETENTION THEORY FOR TEACHERS

"I don't remember" are words that stand as three tombstones commemorating failure, no matter how valiant the effort, in the teaching-learning process. As such, these words are audible reminders that learning from teaching is the result of a delicate, sometimes unpredictable interaction rather than an inevitable cause and effect relationship. How to move toward more predictable success in learning is the never-ending quest of teachers as they engage in the search for methods that are more productive of learning and ways that result more surely in retention of that which has been learned. Paralleling this search effort is a teacher's frequent feeling of frustration from not knowing what really did the trick when a lesson is successfully remembered.

In the last century, research has begun to supply some solutions to these vexing and ever-present problems. As a result, we have mountains of data related to retention, innumerable unanswered questions, some sophisticated hunches, some tenable generalizations, and a few validated principles. It is to the latter we will turn our attention, for understanding only five basic principles provides a formidable armamentarium for the teacher who wishes to attack the problem of "I don't remember" by planning lessons where retention is more probable. Notice we say "more probable" rather than "for sure." With all human endeavors there are so many factors beyond our control that we can never ensure a perfect one-to-one correspondence between what we do and the result of our action. Increasing the probability of desirable results, however, is enough to make any teacher sit up and take notice, for too much of the time we feel the success of our endeavors is dependent on extra sensory perception, divine revelation, or fate.

This programed book on retention theory was designed to introduce you to some factors that you can use tomorrow in your classroom to make remembering more probable and forgetting less likely. One of the first things you as a teacher will have to remember is that you cannot control ALL the factors that have a bearing on memory and, consequently, your students' retention is never guaranteed.

In this book we will 1) present some information about factors that promote retention, 2) give examples to help you see how they work, 3) ask you a question that will necessitate application of your knowledge to a teaching situation, and 4) let you know if your answer is correct. If you are right, you will be directed to the next page that presents more information. If you are wrong, you will be told why and directed back to the question so you can make another choice.

Let's see if you remember what you have read so far.

If you as a teacher wish your students to remember what you have just taught, you should:

a. hope.................................Turn to page 3 top
b. learn about the factors that increase
   retention so you can be sure they
   are present in your lesson..............Turn to page 3 bottom
c. try to discover the one sure way to achieve.
   retention..............................Turn to page 4 top
d. leave it in the hands of fate...........Turn to page 4 bottom

a. You said a teacher should hope.

All of us do, but we'll be disappointed too many times if we do not learn about some of the factors by which we can change our hope into reality. Turn back to page 2 and choose an answer that indicates this.

b. You said you should learn about the factors that increase retention so you can be sure they are present in your lesson.

Right you are! You have shown that you remember well what you learn from reading, so you're ready to turn to page 5 and find out about factors you can work with every day to make retention more probable.

c. You said a teacher should try to discover the one sure way to insure retention.

We're with you, but so far the best efforts of researchers have failed to disclose this magic formula. Until that happy day when you or someone else makes the successful discovery we who teach will need to do something else. Turn back to page 2 and select an answer that may make you successful in the meantime.

d. You said we should leave it in the hands of fate.

We may have to, but only as a last resort. In the meantime, thank goodness, there are some things we can do. Turn back to page 2 and select an answer which will indicate we aren't just sitting on our hands and waiting for something to happen.

As you know, there is no one factor that ensures retention. Each one is dependent on a number of other factors that will assist in promoting memory, or interfere and result in forgetting. We will separate these factors in order to learn about them, but YOUR retention job is to remember that most of them are operating together and interacting all the time.

In the following pages you will be learning about ways to increase retention through 1) *meaning*, 2) *degree of original learning*, 3) *presence of feeling tone*, 4) *positive and negative transfer*, and 5) *schedule of practice*.

MEANING

If we were to select one of the most important yet most neglected factors that promote retention, it would be MEANING. We are more apt to remember material which is meaningful to us than material which has no meaning. Mathematics as it used to be taught is an outstanding violation of this principle of retention. Most of us memorized the long division ritual of our "goes into's" and "bring down's" and the "borrowing" directions of "draw a line through the 8, make it a 7, and put a 1 in front of the 6," to say nothing of the fractional mystery of "invert the divisor and multiply" when we didn't have the foggiest notion of why we were doing any of it. As a result of this lack of meaning in the operations we were performing, we forgot as rapidly as we learned, and a nation of mathaphobes and snarled checkbooks is the result. One of the major purposes of the "new math" was to imbue it with meaning. Unfortunately, all too often this has not been accomplished, and as a result, students are failing to remember. A teacher's lack of understanding can reduce meaning even further for the students.

One of the easiest ways to invest any learning with meaning is to relate it to the learner's own life and experience. Using a difficult word in a sentence containing the learner's name is a powerful but seldom used technique. "Jim, you made a VALIANT effort to help your team win today," not only assists Jim's memory of the word "valiant" but builds his ego as well. Comparing the whole-part relationships of fractions to the similar relationship of members of the learner's family to his whole family, will not only help him learn faster the relationship of parts to a whole but remember it longer.

If you wished a learner to remember that a map is a schematic representation of a portion of the world, you probably should have him begin by:

a. working on a map of his town.............Turn to page 7 top
b. working on a map of the United States. . Turn to page 7 bottom
c. working on a map of the school...........Turn to page 8 top
d. working on a map of a foreign country. . Turn to page 8 bottom

a. You said you would have the student work on a map of his town.

It should have meaning, but you can't be sure he really knows about all the places that are on the map and the spacial relationship of one to the other. If a student hasn't had a chance to go to certain places in town, he probably won't know their directional relationship to the places he has been. Turn back to the question on page 6 and select an answer where you can guarantee places and their relationships are meaningful to him.

b. You said you would have a student work on a map of the United States.

It would be better than choosing Ghana, but unless he has traveled extensively, he has only heard about most of the cities and states; consequently, the relationship of their location has little real meaning for him. Turn back to the question on page 6 and select an answer which represents the maximum meaning for the learner.

c. You said you would have the student work on a map of the school.

Right! If that doesn't have meaning for him, we might as well give up. Should there be places in the school where he hasn't been, you have the opportunity to take him there so any schematic representation will be imbued with real meaning for him. You may even need to "back up" to a map of his present room and then extend it to the school to be sure he perceives the spacial relationship of one to the other. Turn now to page 9 and see how many times our daily practice violates the principle, "the more meaningful the material, the better the retention."

d. You said you would have him work on a map of a foreign country.

After he knew what maps were all about this would be all right. Before he knew they were schematic representations of reality, he might just as well be working on an abstract design, for that is all it would be. Turn back to the question on page 6 and select an answer where the student would be sure to have had direct experience with the area that the map represented.

How many times have you heard, "If he doesn't understand, don't worry; that will come later." There is very little "later" for a student who does not understand something, because learning without meaning is soon forgotten. Think about your own college experience. You probably took a course in psychology that dealt with retention but how much did you retain? If you are like most teachers, your answer would be, "Very little!" You probably read about rat experiments that were well-laced wtih unintelligible statistics and, as a result, you never thought of the whole thing as meaningful to your own teaching. Right? How did we know? Because we took those courses too! On the other hand, your exposure to that psychology course may make this book more meaningful to you, but it was a big price of time to pay. We hope the short time spent on reading this book will accomplish what your psychology course didn't and be much more meaningful; consequently, you should remember it longer.

Your memory of the extensive "fall out" of what you learned in psychology, which had no practical meaning, should make you extra careful that what you teach has real meaning for your students. Don't get caught in the trap of "covering the material" unless you cover it appropriately and lay it to rest. Without meaning it's dead anyway.

If you are teaching U. S. History and you find you are getting behind schedule you probably should:

a. divide the number of pages by the weeks left
   and cover that much each week . . . . Turn to page 10 top
b. assign homework so you can get back on
   schedule . . . . Turn to page 10 bottom
c. go as far as you can and hope for the
   best . . . . Turn to page 11 top
d. select the most important concepts,
   concentrate on them and skip the rest . . Turn to page 11 bottom

9

a. You said you would divide the number of pages by the weeks left and cover that much each week.

You're remembering your mathematics but forgetting your psychology so we doubt if it will help in U. S. History. Not that there aren't thousands of teachers before you who have made the same decision. In fact, it probably happened to you as a student, and as a result, what do you remember about those wars and dates? You have chosen an answer that indicates your feeling of responsibility but not your knowledge of what promotes memory. Turn back to the question on page 9 and select an answer that shows you're as wise as you are responsible.

b. You said you would assign homework so you could get back on schedule.

We wish it would work. Usually it doesn't. Covering material without teacher guidance and interpretation often results in increased confusion which further slows down learning. Homework is fine if it will further something that is already understood. If it is assigned in lieu of teaching, it cannot be counted on to add anything but headaches. As a teacher, you have enough of those without courting them. Turn back to the question on page 9 and select an answer that shows you can make an adjustment that will result in you and your students feeling more comfortable, knowing they have learned the important material.

c. You said you would go as far as you can and hope for the best.

At least you have sense enough to know that you are going to have to make some adjustments. But what about all the non-essential concepts that slow you down along the way? And how are you going to feel when your students have never heard of the important material that comes at the end? Go back to the question on page 9 and select an answer that shows you can make an adjustment that will result in you and your students feeling more comfortable, knowing they have learned the most important material.

d. You said you would select the most important concepts, concentrate on them and skip the rest.

Bravo! You are making valid application of retention theory, to say nothing of wise curricular decisions. By selecting the key concepts and skipping the unimportant details you are probably giving yourself the much-needed time. By concentrating on those key concepts, you are providing the opportunity to imbue them with real meaning for the students. Whether you help students see the similarity of Civil War issues to those that exist in their daily life, or whether you liken their feelings when they quit a game to the feeling of the Southerners as they seceded from the Union, is not important as long as you are sure that what they learn has real meaning for them rather than being rote memorization. Making sure they understand is a giant step toward helping them remember. Your answer shows you understand and will remember. Turn now to page 12.

11

You are no doubt asking, "What about the many routine things that must be remembered like the arithmetic combinations or spelling?" How can you give meaning to this kind of material? Often you can't. The way a word is spelled has meaning only if you are sophisticated in linguistics, and most of us are not. The process of multiplication has meaning, but that is of little help when you must remember all the combinations, to say nothing of the addition, subtraction, and division facts.

Here's where knowledge of retention theory helps, for you are not dependent on any one single factor, but know others that you may use to promote lasting effects from your teaching efforts. After you make sure that as much *meaning* as possible has been incorporated, you can turn to the factors of *degree of original learning, presence of feeling tone, positive and negative transfer, and schedule of practice.*

DEGREE OF ORIGINAL LEARNING

DEGREE OF ORIGINAL LEARNING refers to how well something was learned in the first place. We've all had the embarrassing experience of being introduced to someone only to find a few minutes later we can't remember his name. Usually this is because there was insufficient learning at the first exposure. We can ask his name again, and the knowledge may last through the meeting or social event, but if we have to recall his name a week later, it's all a void. Yet we have little trouble (usually!) remembering the names of our friends we haven't seen recently or the President of the United States whom we have never met. Of course, meaning has a great deal to do with this, but also *amount* of learning is important in determining retention. Rulers of other countries and positions in the U.S. Cabinet have almost as much meaning as the U.S. presidency, but we haven't learned those names as well, if at all. Consequently, we have difficulty remembering them even though we have read or heard the names.

Knowing that amount of original learning is important to retention, we won't waste our students' time by going "once over lightly", but will see that important material is well learned. Giving 20 new spelling words each week and then never reviewing them, reading a chapter of a book and moving on without doing anything about it, seeing a film once and then moving to new content are all examples of daily violation of the principle that the better the original learning, the better the retention.

After you have taught an important lesson, before you move on, we hope you will test or make some kind of assessment to see how much was learned. Should you be disappointed in the results, you probably should:

a. resolve to change your mode of presentation and move on..........................Turn to page 14 top.
b. announce the poor results and give students that evening to study before you give the test again tomorrow ....Turn to page 14 bottom.
c. give a resounding lecture on poor study habits ....Turn to page 15 top.
d. re-teach the lesson ....Turn to page 15 bottom.

a. You said you would resolve to change your mode of presentation and move on.

You are showing that you have learned from the experience, but what about the students? They are supposed to learn too! If as a result of their poor scores you become a better teacher, the future results will show it; but what about the important material that wasn't learned in this lesson? If it was poorly learned, it probably will not be remembered. Unless you're willing to settle for forgetting, you'd better turn back to the question on page 13 and select another answer.

b. You said you would announce the poor results and give students that evening to study before you give the test again tomorrow.

You're catching on to the fact that the material better be learned, but are they catching on? If they didn't learn it with your help, how can you be sure they will do it on their own? Turn back to the question on page 13 and select an answer that shows you know retention is related to amount of original learning, and you plan to do something about that learning.

c. You said you would give a resounding lecture on poor study habits.

If that works, write up the lecture and publish it so we can read your book. We assume you will say things that you hope will make your students learn more in the future, but what about that important material just passed (which they failed)? Unless you're willing to say it was not important enough to remember, you'd better go back to the question on page 13 and select an answer that will make remembering more probable.

d. You said that you would re-teach the lesson.

Good for you! We would hope that looking at the results of the first teaching would suggest ways you could redesign the lesson and teach it differently so it would be more effective. But even if you did the same thing over, paying careful attention to the pacing of the lesson and looking for signs that you weren't coming across, it would probably result in more learning, and therefore longer retention. Now you know that *meaning* and *the amount of original learning* are two important factors in promoting retention. To find out about another factor turn to the next page. (16)

FEELING TONE

The presence of FEELING TONE has a great deal to do with memory. Try to remember one of your worst days of teaching, one you wish you could forget. The memory is only too vivid, isn't it? That's good, because if you couldn't remember any such days it would probably be because you had repressed the memory as being too unpleasant for you to tolerate. Now think of one of your good days, one where a lesson came off extremely well or the students performed in a way that was a credit to your teaching ability. We all wish there were more of these to remember; but you, no doubt, can call many to mind. Now try to remember the details of just an ordinary lesson last week, one that was neither good nor bad, just so-so. It's hard to remember, isn't it?

You have just experienced the practical application of the relation of feeling tone to memory. We remember best those things that are associated with pleasant feeling tone. Next, we remember those things that are associated with unpleasant feeling tones although we may try to eliminate them from our memory by repressing them. We have a difficult time remembering those things that have no feeling tone associated with them.

How do we translate this knowledge into our daily teaching so that what we carefully prepare to be learned is as dependably remembered? First, we make every effort to make learning a pleasantly stimulating and exciting experience. To help a student develop a real zest for learning is the zenith of good teaching, as well as promoting the efficiency of remembering what is learned.

Making learning unpleasant may promote retention, but it is dangerous because it will also promote a lot of other things that are less desirable. We have no trouble remembering unpleasant learning experiences in our own past, but that memory has usually resulted in our avoiding any further learning encounters in that particular content area or with anything or anyone associated with it. Unhappy experiences in math and foreign language have resulted in many students dropping those subjects as soon as possible. Traumatic memories of learning parts of speech or Chaucer have resulted in people who can read and write, but never do if they can possibly avoid it.

16

Neutral feeling tones are useless as far as memory is concerned. A learning experience that is neither pleasant nor unpleasant is soon forgotten. This forgetting at times may be more desirable than remembering with unpleasant feeling tones, because forgetting resulting from neutral feeling tones, is not contaminated with the avoidance of learning that can result from unpleasant feelings. Consequently, a student can comfortably return to a neutral subject for re-learning while he may refuse to return to an unpleasant subject for further learning.

Let's apply our knowledge about the relation of feeling tone to retention as we look at a typical classroom situation.

You want to make sure that students remember important events in history. You decide that to add the retentive power of pleasant feeling tones you will—

a. have the students create a play and re-enact
   the historical events .... Turn to page 18 top.
b. have the students make a notebook collecting materials and illustrations of their choice.... Turn to page 18 bottom.
c. have the students suggest several ways they
   would like to work and let each student make a
   choice from the suggested alternatives..... Turn to page 19 top.
d. provide many kinds of materials and have the
   students select those they need to make dioramas
   of important historical events .... Turn to page 19 bottom.

a. You said you would have the students create a play and re-enact the historical events.

You would probably have some pleasant feeling tones. Anyone who has ever been in a senior play remembers it the rest of his life. There's one important difference, however. Students wanted to be in that senior play or they wouldn't have tried out for a part. You're not sure that every student in the whole class wants to be in a play. And what about all the boys who wanted to be Daniel Boone and didn't get the part? You have the right idea; plays are fun for most, but turn back to the question on page 17 and choose an answer that will more nearly provide pleasant feeling tones for everyone.

b. You said you would have the students make a notebook collecting materials and illustrations of their choice.

Many teachers have, and we're glad you're letting students do some choosing. But think back on the notebooks and term papers you have done and the way you felt about them. If your feelings were pleasant, it no doubt accounts for the reason you choose this answer. But not everyone is like you, so go back to the question on page 17 and choose an answer that will also take care of the non-literary student.

c. You said you would have the students suggest several ways they would like to work and let each student make a choice from the suggested alternatives.

We can't think of anything more pleasant unless it would be forgetting the whole thing and going on a picnic. Your answer indicates you are wise enough to know that only the individual himself can determine what is pleasant for him. What one person enjoys, the other may not be able to tolerate. Whenever you give a learner a choice of alternatives, you have added the critical dimension of his knowledge of what is pleasant for him plus the dividend of being in charge of his own fate, which is pleasant for all of us. You're in charge of your fate, so if you choose to turn to page 20 you will find out more about retention.

d. You said you would provide many kinds of materials and have the students select those they need to make dioramas of important historical events.

You are giving students some choice, which is always pleasant. Also, you are letting them create with their hands and minds, which is pleasant unless you're a bumble fingers. But what about those students who find creation with words or with a paint brush more pleasant? Use your good idea of choice and turn back to the questions on page 17 to select an answer more likely to create pleasant feeling tones for everyone.

19

We have talked about making learning as *meaningful* as possible, achieving as much *mastery of that learning* as possible, all in a *pleasant* atmosphere. You are, of course, aware that all of these go together. If you really understand something, you will learn it better, and that's a pleasant feeling. If you are trying to learn something you don't understand, it is difficult, you don't learn it as well, and it's unpleasant, so you may abandon it to make your feeling neutral. If you try to recall it later you find you've forgotten most of it.

So far we haven't said anything you didn't already know, have we? Of course, you may not have given these factors which are so important in retention the same names we've used—*meaning, degree of learning,* and *feeling tones.* Still in this book it's been very easy for you to learn and remember these labels because they describe the situations you have encountered in classroom teaching. These factors have a great deal of *meaning* for you. You know them well, so you have achieved a *desirable degree of learning.* Your *feelings* of adequacy as a teacher are associated with students remembering or forgetting what you've taught, so your feelings will help you remember these factors which are so important in promoting retention.

If you have never taught, or had the experience of trying to get a learner to remember, it will not be so easy for you to remember these factors because the examples are not so *meaningful* to you. As a result, you may not have achieved a *desirable degree of learning.* Because you have neither feelings of success nor of failure, your *feeling* tones are neutral. Your past teaching experience, or lack of it, makes an important difference in the amount of meaning, degree of learning, and feeling tone this book has for you, and consequently in your retention of this material. For you and all learners past experience can either help or hinder retention. We'll look first at the way past learning can help.

20

POSITIVE TRANSFER

When other learnings in your past experience help you learn and remember something in the present, we call this POSITIVE TRANS-FER. Something you have already learned fits well with the new learning so it helps you acquire and remember a new learning. For example, if you know how to teach children of one age, it is easier for you to learn to teach children of different ages, than it is for a person who has never taught. If you play a violin, it is easier for you to learn to play a cello, than it is for a piano player to learn to play a cello. If you understand base ten in math, it is easier for you to learn to work in base two, than a person who doesn't understand base at all.

The more similar learnings are, the more we get transfer from one to the other. To increase this transfer, we teach the new by pointing out its similarity to the already learned.

If we wish a person's ability to teach kindergarteners to transfer to his ability to teach college students, we would stress that the latter will remember better if we observe the same principles of retention, which worked so well with kindergarteners.

If we wish a violin player to learn to play a cello, we would increase transfer of musical skill by emphasizing the ways the two instruments were similar.

If a student knows base ten, we would increase transfer to base two by emphasizing the similarity to previously learned place-value concepts.

Whenever the transfer of old learning to new learning assists the new learning, we call it *positive transfer*, and this factor will aid in the retention of new learning.

If a student really understands Roman numerals, which of these new lessons would you expect him to remember longer as a result of positive transfer?

a. learning numeration systems that are
   different from ours ....Turn to page 22 top.
b. applying addition and subtraction facts
   to word problems...................Turn to page 22 bottom.
c. learning how to multiply and divide......Turn to page 23 top.
d. learning how to add and subtract .....Turn to page 23 bottom.

a. You said you would expect positive transfer from knowing Roman numerals to learning numeration systems that are different from ours.

Right you are! The knowledge that different symbols can be used to represent numbers, that not all numeration systems use the same place value, and that ways of representing quantity differ, are all learnings that apply to Roman numerals and to other numeration systems. Consequently, this knowledge will assist the student in learning and remembering new numeration systems. Because the old knowledge *assists* the acquiring and remembering of new knowledge, it is positively transferring to the new learning and memory task. Of course, you will also recognize that the previous learning will add *meaning* to the new learning because both are instances of the same generalizations. Turn now to page 24.

b. You said you would expect positive transfer from Roman numerals to applying addition and subtraction facts to word problems.

You might get a little transfer for you are adding and subtracting when you work with Roman numerals. Still in most word problems you are working in base ten and may be carrying and regrouping. You do not do this in Roman numerals and will get in trouble if you try. Go back to the question on page 21 and select an answer where what a student knows about Roman numerals will help him learn and remember the new lesson.

c. You said you would expect positive transfer from Roman numerals to learning how to multiply and divide.

If there was pleasant feeling tone in learning Roman numerals, you might get some positive transfer because the student would anticipate the new lesson would also be enjoyable; however, the same statement could be made about any previous encounter with math. We were looking for some specific learning from Roman numerals that would transfer and help the new learning. In Roman numerals you use no multiplication and division, so there is no skill in these operations to transfer. Go back to the question on page 21 and see if you can locate an answer that will take advantage of already learned generalizations from Roman numerals.

d. You said you would expect positive transfer from Roman numerals to learning how to add and subtract.

The reverse might be true. You would certainly expect the knowledge of addition and subtraction to transfer into remembering how to write Roman numerals. If you didn't already know these processes, you would have a mighty difficult time knowing how to make XII or IV. Go back to the question on page 21 and select an answer where the knowledge transferring from Roman numerals will assist retention in the new lesson.

What you have just learned about positive transfer is an important reason behind all the new curricula which stress the teaching of generalizations rather than facts. Learning one fact will usually not help you to learn or remember another. Generalizations are important because of their wide applicability. Consequently, you can achieve a great deal of positive transfer from the memory of any generalization.

For example, remembering that a whale is a mammal is of no use in determining whether a new animal is or is not. Learning the generalization that "mammals are characterized by _____ _____ _____" is useful in sorting out all the animals that are mammals (possess those characteristics) from animals that are not. How much more effective is the learning of this generalization than the memorization of factual lists of animals that are mammals. Only by knowing the determining characteristics of mammals will you achieve positive transfer so that in a new situation you can apply the generalization to categorize an unknown animal.

Which of the following statements will yield the greatest positive transfer to you as a teacher so you remember how to help your students' memory?

a. memorizing the parts of speech will positively transfer to writing correctly.............Turn to page 25 top.
b. rigorous learning in one field will train the mind for learning in another..........Turn to page 25 bottom.
c. positive transfer will aid retention........Turn to page 26 top.
d. if two learnings are based on the same generalization, you should get positive transfer from one to the other.........Turn to page 26 bottom.

a. You said that the statement, "memorizing the parts of speech will positively transfer to writing correctly," would help *you* remember how to help your students' memory.

We'll bet that there are plenty of unpleasant feeling tones connected with both learning and teaching the parts of speech, and that may have something to do with your memory and consequent choice of this statement. Unfortunately, it is not true. You can know all the parts of speech and still be a terrible writer. Besides how does the statement help with remembering math, social studies, spelling, and science? Go back to the question on page 24 and select an answer that is true and will positively transfer to any learning situation.

b. You said that the statement, "rigorous learning in one field will train the mind for learning in another," would help *you* remember how to help your students' memory.

A lot of people used to think that was true. Recently, however, we have learned that the way of thinking in the two fields must be similar, or they may actually interfere with each other. A person trained in the precision of one field, such as engineering, may have difficulty with the ambiguity that is necessary in another, such as a behavioral science. Go back to the question on page 24 and select an answer that would imply the similarity necessary for positive transfer.

c. You said that the statement, "positive transfer will aid retention," would help you remember how to help your students' memory.

If you understand why this is so, you're in business; but you would have selected a different answer. There is one that will help *you* a great deal more to remember how to help your students remember. Go back to the question on page 24 and select that answer.

d. You said that the statement, "if two learnings are based on the same generalization, you should get positive transfer from one to the other," would help you remember how to help your students' memory.

Absolutely correct! This knowledge should make you always seek the fundamental principle in back of any fact or event. This can yield positive transfer to other facts and events based on the same principle and help learning and remembering the new ones. Knowing that a child has no difficulty remembering his name because it has real meaning for him, should transfer to help *you* remember to be sure other names must have real meaning, if they are to be remembered (rather than a series of names and dates from a chapter in a book). Knowing that pleasant feeling tones aid memory of a picnic should transfer to help you remember to make learning pleasant for your students. Knowing that material must be well learned if it is to be remembered should transfer to make you remember to be resistant to the temptation of any "once over lightly" lessons. Knowledge of the retention generalizations in back of lessons that are successfully remembered should positively transfer to all the lessons you plan so they will be remembered. Turn now to page 27.

We have been talking about knowledge in one situation that we want to transfer to another situation. What about knowledge we *don't* want to transfer? Your memory of one friend's phone number may transfer to the memory of another friend's number with a resultant wrong number scramble. The memory of "i before e" may transfer to your spelling of "neither." Your memory of the location of the lights and windshield wiper on your old car may transfer to your new car with the result that you pull the wrong knob and unexpected things happen.

NEGATIVE TRANSFER

Whenever the memory of one learning interferes with another, we call this NEGATIVE TRANSFER. To avoid this undesirable interference, we make certain learnings as different as possible. The more similar things are, the more we get transfer from one to another. Consequently, if we wish *positive* transfer, we teach things together and we stress similarities. To avoid *negative* transfer, we do not teach certain things together and we stress differences. To illustrate, if we want a learner's knowledge of the word "want" to transfer to his knowledge of "wants" and "wanting," we present the words together stressing the parts that are the same. On the other hand, we wish to avoid negative transfer with the possible interference of "want" and "went" so we teach these words separately, stressing the difference in meaning so each will be remembered as different from the other. We bring them together *only* if children are confusing them and we need to emphasize the difference between the 'a' and the 'e'. In this case we are teaching the cue so one word may be discriminated from the other.

When we teach a spelling rule, we use only the words that conform to the rule. In that way, we will get the positive transfer that is appropriate. Not until these words are well learned so they will be well remembered do we introduce the exceptions to the rule. Even then, we may get negative transfer and both conforming words and exceptions may be misspelled. If so, we must again separate them and reteach each group without the other. We bring them together only if we need to stress how they are different.

27

Knowing that the memory of one learning will transfer to the memory of similar learnings is a very important generalization for teachers. This knowledge should keep us from getting negative transfer by making the mistake of teaching:

a. 7 x 9 followed by 8 x 8.................Turn to page 29 top.
b. 7 x 9 followed by 9 x 7..............Turn to page 29 bottom.
c. 6 x 4 followed by 6 x 8 ....Turn to page 30 top.
d. 3 x 3 followed by 3 x 9..............Turn to page 30 bottom.

a. You said we would get negative transfer by teaching 7 x 9 followed by 8 x 8.

Right! The answers of 63 and 64 are too much alike. Both of these answers are dependent on memory more than meaning. Consequently, we should have attained a considerable degree of learning with one before we proceed to the other. If this was your first choice for answering our question, you are very perceptive for you looked beyond your own actions as a teacher, which was presenting the problem, and used your knowledge to analyze the learner's answer. *This is so important that we included this question to emphasize the fact that a teacher must always anticipate the learner's response as one of the most important factors in transfer.* If you didn't answer our question correctly on your first choice, your response was what *we* anticipated. We hoped you would make an error so the addition of the slightly unpleasant feeling tone of being wrong would assist your memory of *always anticipating the learner's response* (in this case the answer) to see if you are running the risk of negative transfer. Turn now to page 31 to see if you can answer a more difficult question involving transfer.

b. You said we would get negative transfer by teaching 7 x 9 followed by 9 x 7.

The opposite should be true. They are based on the same generalization so we should expect positive transfer. That is why in current math teaching we present the two together so the memory of one will aid the memory of the other. Turn back to the question on page 28 and select an answer where the memory of the answer to the first combination will interfere with the memory of the second.

c. You said we would get negative transfer by teaching 6 x 4 followed by 6 x 8.

If we teach with meaning, we should get some positive transfer. A learner who understands the relationship of 4 to 8 should find it easier to remember the answers of 24 and 48 if he perceives they have the same relationship as 4 and 8. This similarity should yield *positive* transfer. Turn back to the question on page 28 and choose an answer where the similarity will interfere with remembering the correct answers.

d. You said we would get negative transfer by teaching 3 x 3 followed by 3 x 9.

If we teach with meaning, we should get some *positive* transfer. A learner who understands the relationship of 3 to 9 should find it easier to remember the answers of 9 and 27, for he should perceive they have the same relationship. This similarity should yield positive transfer. Turn back to the question on page 28 and choose an answer where the similarity will interfere with remembering the correct answers.

30

Suppose you find your students are confused about which column to add first when they do addition. You decide to reteach and stress "always add the ones first and then add the tens." Which example should they practice first to minimize negative transfer?

a. 17 + 3 = ...Turn to page 32 top.
b. 21 + 73 = ...Turn to page 32 bottom.
c. 15 + 13 = ...Turn to page 33 top.
d. 10 + 10 = ...Turn to page 33 bottom.

a. You said they should first practice 17 + 3 =.

This would be fine if they already knew which numbers to add first. If they are just learning, our guess is that you would get negative transfer from their previous association of ones and tens with the numerals rather than with positions related to place value. As a result, "add the ones first" could mean the numeral "1" in "17". If they knew 7 + 3 = 10, they could think "add the tens last" meant that. Turn back to page 31 and select an example that would eliminate this possible negative transfer.

b. You said they should first practice 21 + 73 =.

Right you are! By associating the one's place with their previous knowledge of the numeral "1", you are eliminating any possible confusion with a numeral "1" when it represents a ten because it is in the ten's place, as in 13, 14, 15, etc.

If you are thinking that having children remember "add the ones first and then the tens" is a poor way to teach math, you are absolutely right. They are depending on rote memory rather than meaning. If you apply retention theory correctly and concentrate on the meaning of place value in base ten, you probably would never have had the problem and needed to reteach in the first place. Now turn to page 34.

c. You said you should first practice $15 + 13 =$.

This would be fine if they already knew which numerals to add first. If they are just learning, our guess is that they would get negative transfer from their previous association of ones and tens with the numerals rather than with positions related to place value. As a result, "add the ones first" could mean the numeral "1" in the numbers 15 and 13 which is just the opposite of what you are trying to teach. Also, they could think $5 + 3 = 8$ which is more like 10 than $1 + 1$, so they had better add them last. Turn back to page 31 and choose an answer that would eliminate this possible negative transfer.

d. You said they should first practice $10 + 10 =$.

The first question you are apt to get is, "Where are the ones we are supposed to add first?" Not seeing them, they may assume the numeral "1" in the number 10 is where they are supposed to begin, which is just the opposite of what you are trying to teach. They may even assume that the number ten has a zero, so use that as identification of the column they add last. Turn back to page 31 and select an example that will eliminate this possible negative transfer.

If you want learnings to transfer, stress the sameness of the principles involved in those learnings and bring examples together. If you do *not* want them to transfer, keep them apart. If there is confusion, bring them together only to stress their differences or unlikeness. It is as if you were working with two colors of paint; if you want them to mix, put them together and one will run into the other. If you don't want them to mix, keep them separated.

Suppose you wish students to learn the difference between fact and opinion as they read the newspaper. Most students have learned to discriminate between fact and fiction, the one being true and the other not true. The concept of fiction (not being true) is of no help at all in discriminating between fact and opinion. Therefore, if fiction is brought into the learning situation, it will interfere with the development of discrimination between fact and opinion. Consequently, at no time while you are beginning to teach the difference between facts and opinion is a fictitious statement introduced. Discrimination between fact and opinion is developed by such statements as "Mrs. Brown was at the gathering" versus "Mrs. Brown was the most beautiful woman at the gathering." Negative transfer from the already learned fact-fiction discrimination would result from statements of "Mrs. Brown was at the gathering" versus "Mrs. Brown was *not* at the gathering."

In teaching the difference of fact and opinion, negative transfer could also result from the previous learning of consensus and agreement. The concept of a fact as something everyone would agree to, i.e., "Mrs. Brown is a woman" can become confused with consensus, i.e., "Everyone agreed Mrs. Brown wore the most beautiful dress." Consequently, the idea of consensus or everyone having the same opinion will yield negative transfer and consequent interference with learning and memory, if it is brought into the initial stages of learning, to discriminate between fact and opinion.

If we have done a good job in writing this program, you will remember that memory is increased in relation to the amount of meaning, presence of feeling tone, degree of original learning, and positive transfer.

Very well, you think, if the student really understands and can relate it to something in his own life, it has meaning. If I as a teacher make my lessons stimulating and fun, they will have pleasant feeling

34

tone. If I teach the basic generalizations and concepts underlying the content, positive transfer will assist memory of new content. If I am aware of possible negative transfer, I can avoid it. I must be sure not to focus on merely covering the material; it must be well learned or it will be forgotten. But how do the students arrive at that well-learned state?

PRACTICE

This is an excellent question and one that has confounded educators since the beginning of time. Meaning, feeling tone, and positive transfer will contribute to that "well-learned state," but it may also take PRACTICE. The relation of practice to retention is more complex than doing something again and again and again. Successful planned practice involves decisions of "how much," "how many times," and "how often." Translated into the learning of a poem, it means 1) how much of the poem should you try to remember in one practice period; the whole poem, one stanza, four lines, or one line? 2) how many times should you go over it or how long should the practice period be; one hour, one-half hour, ten minutes, or five minutes? 3) how often should you have practice periods; five times a day, once a day, every other day, or once a week?

Let's take these questions separately. How much should you try to learn at one time? Generally, you should learn the *smallest part that still maintains adequate meaning*. Usually one line of a poem does not have adequate meaning. Consequently, you would need to learn several lines that go together or a whole stanza. This is usually more efficient and will result in faster learning and longer memory than trying to learn the whole poem at one time unless it is very short.

In contrast to poetry where each line of a stanza adds meaning to the other lines, most addition, subtraction, and multiplication combinations add little meaning to each other. 5 + 4 will probably interfere with, rather than enhance the meaning of 9 + 8. Consequently, very small amounts of number combinations are usually more efficient. (You will notice all through this book you will find "usually," "probably," "should," and "will likely." Remember that we can never control all the variables in human learning so you can *probably* find an exception to anything we say.)

If you are trying to remember the causes of a war, the characteristics of a species, or the factors promoting retention, your memory will be aided by taking them in the smallest amounts that will preserve meaningful relationships. The causes of the war might be divided into geographic, historic, political, etc., and each learned as a smaller unit before putting them together. The characteristics of a species might be grouped by skeletal, neural, glandular, etc. You have already learned the factors in retention separately by considering meaning, feeling tone, transfer, amount of original learning, and practice. Even though all of these interact, each has meaning by itself so learning them separately and then putting them together should increase the efficiency of your remembering them.

If you are trying to teach the multiplication facts and wish to promote the greatest retention, you would have students work a short time on:

a. any facts they don't know . . . . Turn to page 37 top
b. just one set such as the 9's . . . . Turn to page 37 bottom
c. one or two difficult combinations . . . . Turn to page 38 top
d. their 7's, 8's, and 9's . . . . Turn to page 38 bottom

a. **You said you would have students work on any facts they don't know.**

If they knew most of them this might be effective, for there would be few to learn. Even then they would probably confuse several answers unless they were grouped meaningfully. If students were just beginning to learn their combinations, they would encounter an impossible memory maze. Multiplication facts are more meaningful after you know them than they are while you are learning. Consequently, you should take small learning "bites" rather than the whole rich diet. Go back to the question on page 36 and select an answer that incorporates the idea.

b. **You said you would have students work on just one set such as the 9's.**

It sounds reasonable, doesn't it? That's what most teachers have been doing since the beginning of time. You know only too well the results. That is why we are writing a program on retention. There are nine different facts to be learned in each set and that is too many when each one is not necessary to the meaning of the other. As a result, you will get a lot of negative transfer with resultant wrong answers. Go back to the question on page 36 and select an answer that will minimize scrambled answers.

c. You said you would have students work on one or two difficult combinations.

You're a wise teacher, and you're correctly applying retention theory. If you select two combinations that are related so each increases the meaning of the other, you're even better. Learning 8 x 4 and 8 x 8 together is meaningful. Learning 8 x 7 and 8 x 9 together could result in interference. Many short practice periods on one or two combinations will make their retention more probable. Now turn to page 39 to find out how to schedule these practice sessions.

d. You said you would have students work on their 7's, 8's, and 9's.

Machines are fast replacing people who have done just that. We don't think you really chose this one, you're just reading it to see what we have to say. What you suspect is true—working on this many combinations will result in so much interference, one with the other, that very little except dislike of multiplication will be learned. Turn back to the question on page 36 and choose an answer that minimizes confusion and interference.

Assuming you have taken the smallest amount of learning that still has meaning, how long should you work on it at one time? Usually many short practice periods are more effective than a few long periods. Of course, this is assuming that the short periods are long enough to get something done. To work on a stanza of a poem for a few minutes at three different times is usually much more effective than one 15-minute practice period. Drill on unrelated learnings such as spelling words or number combinations, where one learning does not enhance the meaning of the next, should usually be scheduled in several short periods during the day rather than one long period. Having a student drill on his multiplication facts for a half hour can be a waste of twenty-five minutes. Of course, the periods must not be so short that nothing is accomplished.

To ensure students' retention of the spelling demons which procedure would you choose?

a. writing a short paragraph using the
spelling demons to emphasize meaning. . . . Turn to page 40 top
b. writing each one correctly 20 times. . . . Turn to page 40 bottom
c. writing the same one or two correctly
several times during the day. . . . . Turn to page 41 top
d. writing them for a 20-minute period
every day. . . . . Turn to page 41 bottom

a. You said you would have students write a short paragraph using the spelling demons to emphasize meaning.

Meaning is important in retention, but we assume the students know what the words mean; it's how they are spelled that is giving them problems. Consequently, our purpose is to provide adequate practice in writing the demons correctly. Using them once in a paragraph will not provide this kind of practice. Go back to the question on page 39 and select an answer that will provide the needed practice in spelling.

b. You said you would have the students write each one correctly 20 times.

It would be nice if it would work—usually it doesn't. In fact, often this kind of practice becomes so mechanical it's easy to repeat an error twenty times without noticing. Don't count on retention from this kind of practice (except remembering how boring spelling can be). Go back to the question on page 39 and select an answer that will provide practice with students paying attention to what they're doing.

c. You said you would have the students write the same one or two correctly several times during the day.

You are remembering your retention theory. You are capitalizing on students' focus on what they are doing, repeating it at frequent intervals so it won't be forgotten, selecting a small enough task so you won't get interference, and applying valid psychological theory to the solution of a difficult learning problem. Turn now to page 42 to find out how to keep your students' memory active.

d. You said you would have the students write the demons for a 20-minute period every day.

It's a laudable resolution but may not be very productive. If they write each one once, little will be remembered. If they write one or two 20 times you are apt to get the same result. The practice period is too long. Spelling one word does not enhance the rationality of spelling another and 24 hours between practice periods allows too much forgetting. Go back to the question on page 39 and select an answer that will take care of all these problems.

We now know we should practice on the smallest amount that has maximum meaning and that several short practice periods are usually better than one long one, providing there is enough time in the short period to accommodate the particular learning task.

This brings us to our third question, how often should we practice and how much time should there be between practice periods? At the *beginning* of any learning, practice periods should be close together. You will remember that material that is not well learned is forgotten rapidly. At the beginning of any learning, the material is not well learned; consequently, it will need to be reviewed frequently to prevent forgetting. A new learning should be reviewed several times the first few days. This is called *massed practice* and refers to the fact that practice periods are close together in time. Massing practice results in fast learning for there are short intervals between practices; consequently, there is not much time for the "fall out" of forgetting.

Once something has been learned we begin to extend the time between practice periods. Possibly we review twice the first day, once the second day, skip the third day, review the fourth day, skip the fifth and sixth days, review the seventh, skip a week, review, etc. This kind of a schedule, where the time between practice periods is increased, is called *distributed practice*. It refers to the fact that we are distributing our practice periods over a long period of time rather than massing our practice in a short period of time. Once something has been learned, distributing practice usually ensures longer retention.

The important generalization for you to remember is: *Mass practice at the beginning of a learning, then distribute practice.* The massing of practice makes for fast learning; distributing practice makes that learning endure.

In this program we have tried to practice what we have just preached. We took the smallest segments of retention theory which had meaning for you as a teacher. These were the factors that were related to retention: meaning, feeling tone, amount of original learning, transfer, and schedule of practice. All of these are interrelated; but it was meaningful to learn about them separately, and it made a smaller unit for you to learn and remember. We massed the practice for each factor by writing several pages about it and then asking you

42

questions. After you had demonstrated that you had learned by answering the question correctly, we distributed our practice. We moved to another factor, but while we were discussing the new factor, we reviewed the old one to give you that distributed practice. (Were you aware we were doing it?) Hopefully, by now, you will remember all five of the factors that are related to retention.

Let's see if you do. If you wish what you teach to be remembered, what are five things you can do?

1. _____

2. _____

3. _____

4. _____

5. _____

If you said something that meant you would:

1. provide maximum meaning,
2. try to achieve pleasant feeling tones,
3. provide for an adequate degree of learning,
4. maximize positive transfer, minimize negative transfer,
5. schedule practice so it is massed at the beginning and then distributed,

you have achieved the objective of this book on retention theory. Practicing remembering what you want to remember is one of the best ways of remembering it.

You have just experienced an excellent way to practice remembering something, which is by taking a test on the material. Testing is one of the best ways of providing motivated practice for the learner because a person taking a test usually tries very hard to remember. Unfortunately, many tests are not given for the purpose of helping a student remember but are designed for the purpose of catching "sinners" who have not learned or have forgotten. As a result, tests often become associated with unpleasant feeling tones. This should not be so. Think of a time when you did very well on a test. We hope it was on the last question we asked. Wasn't it a pleasant feeling?

Weren't you satisfied and pleased by your performance? If we do a good job of teaching and then give a fair test as motivated practice (rather than the arrival of judgment day when your sins have finally caught up with you) we will have achieved pleasant feeling tones plus excellent motivated practice which should promote retention.

When you plan a test to give this desirable motivated practice, don't forget that important variable, meaning. Asking minute, detailed questions about unimportant aspects of the material will minimize meaning. Examples of such questions are often those which can be answered by one word such as a name, date, place, battle, or number. This is not to say that these facts are not necessary aspects of knowledge of the subject, but one fact must be related to others to maximize meaning. One fact in isolation contributes little to retention; consequently, research indicates it is the facts that are first forgotten; meaningful generalizations are longest remembered.

Tests should be designed to emphasize knowledge of major principles or generalizations. In this way, additional motivated practice is provided in the area that is most important to be retained. Meaning is maximized. Positive transfer should result from these generalizations. Pleasant feeling tone comes from dealing with important ideas rather than trying to remember irritating trivia. The motivated practice from a well-designed test should increase the degree of learning. All of these factors contribute significantly to remembering the material learned.

Retention theory now should have meaning for you. We hope it has been pleasant as we have identified important generalizations and used familiar examples so your past experience in teaching would positively transfer to your learning from our examples. We hope we have eliminated any negative transfer that might interfere with your retention. By answering correctly our last question, you have demonstrated achievement of an adequate degree of learning. Your reading of this program has probably been at one or two sittings so your practice has been massed. To ensure retention, you may need to distribute your practice by reviewing these factors as you teach and by referring back to this book to be sure you haven't forgotten any of them.

Just remember not to forget to use your knowledge of the five generalizations about retention so your students will remember.

RETENTION THEORY SELF-TEST

If you wish to give yourself some additional "motivated practice," see if you think we have designed a good test so you can check your memory about forgetting.

1. Which statement should you most easily remember?
   a. $b + d = m$
   b. A teacher can deliberately plan lessons so they are better remembered.
   c. Forgetting is inversely correlated with meaning.
   d. Ebbinghaus experimented with memory in the last century.
   e. Retroactive inhibition is one explanation for forgetting.

2. So children will remember what the Pledge of Allegiance means, you would have them:
   a. say it every morning
   b. use a dictionary to look up definition of key words in the Pledge
   c. memorize the definitions of key words in the Pledge
   d. rewrite the Pledge using their own words to maintain its general meaning
   e. study the lives of American heroes

3. If you were planning the most efficient way for your students to remember that $8 \times 7 = 56$, you would:
   a. practice it once every day
   b. practice on one day for a half hour
   c. practice it whenever it was needed in a problem
   d. concentrate on it until everyone knew it and then spend no more time on it
   e. practice it at closely spaced intervals, and after it was learned, gradually increase the intervals between practice periods on subsequent days

4. Which of the following should be remembered longer?
   a. Why a war was fought
   b. When a war was fought
   c. Where a war was fought
   d. Who were the important generals
   e. What were the important battles

5. To increase retention a teacher should be sure to:
    a. Cover the material included in a course
    b. Spend extra time on the important parts
    c. Make sure that what is taught is thoroughly learned before moving on
    d. Give plenty of drill
    e. Give many tests

6. If all of the following were equally well learned which would probably be best remembered?
    a. All reptiles are cold blooded
    b. Some snakes are ten feet long
    c. A rattlesnake has a diamond pattern
    d. Rattlesnakes are found in certain states
    e. Some snakes like milk

7. Most people can remember the details of their first flight on an airplane. This is probably because:
    a. it was the first time they had done it
    b. there was no negative transfer from another experience
    c. it had a great deal of meaning attached to it
    d. it had a great deal of feeling tone attached to it
    e. it was a well-learned experience

8. Adults know little about the parts of speech although most studied them in school. This is probably because:
    a. they didn't have enough practice
    b. their learning was connected with unpleasant feeling tones
    c. the parts of speech had little real meaning
    d. subsequent learning has interfered with the memory
    e. their original learning was inadequate

9. People often transpose numerals when they are remembering a phone number. This is probably due to:
    a. lack of meaning
    b. negative transfers
    c. insufficient practice
    d. neutral feeling tones
    e. insufficient original learning

10. Students diligently worked on the multiplication facts until by Christmas everyone knew them perfectly. They then used the time to work on other things. Just before Easter vacation a review test revealed students had forgotten many facts. This was probably because:
    a. lack of adequate degree of learning
    b. lack of feeling tone
    c. lack of meaning
    d. lack of positive transfer
    e. lack of distributed practice

11. If you cannot remember what you had for dinner a week ago last Thursday, it is probably due to:
    a. negative transfer
    b. negative feeling tones
    c. positive transfer
    d. positive feeling tones
    e. neutral feeling tones

12. If you went to a foreign country where you never heard or spoke a word of English for five years and then returned to the United States, you would soon remember all your English. This would probably be a result of:
    a. pleasant feeling tones
    b. positive transfer
    c. degree of original learning
    d. distributed practice
    e. massed practice

13. Which of the following would you teach separately to avoid negative transfer?
    a. "some," "thing," and "something"
    b. "was" and "saw"
    c. "go" and "going"
    d. "where" and "somewhere"
    e. "child" and "children"

14. Well designed tests are valuable in promoting retention because they:
    a. identify what has been well learned
    b. identify what has not been learned
    c. alert the teacher to how students' learning is progressing
    d. cause the students to practice remembering
    e. are based on important generalizations

15. When new teachers do not know what to do in a learning situation, they usually revert back to what their teacher did when they were students, rather than remembering and using the theory they learned in college or in-service courses. This is probably due to:
    a. lack of meaning in those courses
    b. lack of appropriate practice with the theory
    c. negative transfer from their past schooling
    d. inadequate learning from the courses
    e. boredom or neutral feeling tones

CORRECT ANSWERS

If you miss one, re-read the section indicated in parenthesis.

1. b (meaning)
2. d (meaning)
3. e (practice)
4. a (meaning)
5. c (degree of original learning)
6. a (positive transfer)
7. d (feeling tone)
8. c (meaning)
9. b (negative transfer)
10. e (practice)
11. e (feeling tone)
12. c (degree of original learning)
13. b (negative transfer)
14. d (practice)

15. *Whatever you answered, you are absolutely right! We hope this programed book is a productive step toward improved teacher education.*
Let us know, will you?

Printed in the United States
60019LVS00002B/2

9 780803 963160